How to Make People Think You're Normal

Ben Goode

Illustrated by
David Mecham

The Truth Abou

Published by:
Apricot Press
Box 1611
American Fork, Utah
84003

books@apricotpress.com
www.apricotpress.com

ISBN 1-885027-14-1

Cover Design & Layout by David Mecham
Printed in the United States of America

Forward

(A completely unrelated introduction to get you in the proper mood...)

How to relieve stress:

-Go on a long vacation to the bathroom.

-Lay in the gutter and let relaxing water flow over you.

-Resolve that whenever anyone tells you to have a nice day, you will vent your frustration by yelling: "Don't tell me what to do!"

-Ignore everything going on around you and stare blankly out the window, while visualizing steak and lobster.

-Make your "To Do" list and fill it with things you've already done.

-Pay the collection agency in pennies.

-Put on boxing gloves and spend an hour pummeling your boss's cat.

-Make every one of your planner pages into paper airplanes; go to the roof of your building, and one-at-a-time, see how far you can sail them.

-During every conversation you have today, resolve that you will hang gummy worms out your nose. (This may relieve others' stress too.)

-Disconnect your computer keyboard and use it to surf down 10 flights of stairs.

-Smear cream all over your body and lay in a dark room filled with cats.

-Use your pent-up stress-energy to figure out how to do the Macarena backwards.

-Answer the phone all day by saying, "I'm sorry, we are not in. Please leave a message after the tone." Then, leave no tone.

-Fill your cubicle with M&Ms and dive in.

-Practice drooling down your shirt.

Contents

1 What is Normal?

What is normal? This is a rhetorical question often asked by rhetoricians who apparently want to know the answer. Most normal people are intent on, even obsessed with, being normal. Being the compassionate journalist I am, I feel it should be my job to eliminate confusion, but since that may not be normal or even possible, I figure I can at least spread some joy and happiness by helping the world think that being confused is normal.

For example, experts[1] tell us the average man is five feet nine inches tall and weighs 160 pounds. That means being six-foot-one would make you abnormal, especially

---

[1] The only expert we know is Jack. So, if you are average, maybe you know Jack. If you are not, it could be said that you don't know Jack.

if you are a girl. I know this is true, too, because I am a guy who happens to be six-feet one-inch tall and for my entire life, I have been told I am as normal as a six year old's dreams after a muppet movie. I am, however, confused about all this, which, as we have documented above, we now consider normal.

The Normal Range

Normal people can hear a pitch between low "D" on the piano and high, high "E". If you have grown older and you can no longer hear normal pitch, I guess you would now have to be considered "abnormal" or "below normal," or better yet, "mutated," since, evolving out of the normal range as you grow older I'm told, is "normal." I even suspect that my hearing has dropped below the normal range, with exception of the voices in my head, which seem to actually be getting louder, and clearer.

While a normal, sane person would go, "whoa, that's horrible," a normal terrorist actually expects to do things like fly airplanes into buildings and poison innocent women and children. The government understands that this behavior is normal for a terrorist; therefore, they are trying to kill the terrorists, which, according to statistics, is normal for governments. The question is then asked, "Does this mean that normal people would be abnormal terrorists, or that terrorists are abnormal, normal people, or that people become abnormal when they go to work for the government?" Whoa! Slow down a minute. Trying to figure this out makes me confused, which, thankfully, as we established earlier, can be considered normal.

Normal people drive Toyotas and nails. If you drive a Rolls Royce, we would have to consider you abnormal. Also, I'm told it's normal, having failed once, to quit trying. Therefore, if you are persistent and determined, you should probably consider yourself abnormal or possibly obnoxious. Normal people complain incessantly, so if I'm not a whiner, could I still consider myself normal? It seems to me that normal people generally dislike or distrust abnormal people. They try everything imaginable to make them normal, or else make them go away. I guess that makes normal people like normal terrorists in that one way.

I am the supreme expert on the subject and ironically, the more I talk about this concept of normal, the more confused I become. I can only imagine how confused you laymen are. If you are normal, it's probably best if you stop trying to figure all this out, because it could make you crazy, which, unless you are a terrorist or a referee, is considered abnormal. I suppose we should also try to figure out if it is normal for normal people to hope terrorists accidentally inhale their own anthrax so that eventually death would become a normal state for a terrorist. There is so much to consider.

Normal vs. Average

This would probably be a good place to draw a distinction between normal and average. Do not get the two concepts mixed up. I can best illustrate the difference by using teenagers as an example. Unfortunately, I can't think of a way to illustrate this concept using teenagers which would not confuse you even worse, so hopefully, you will be content with the knowledge that teenagers are often average, but very rarely normal. Hence, as you can probably guess, the average state of teen parents is nuts, which state (that would either be the state of being nuts or the state of Oregon, take your pick) is probably average for a parent, but which cannot be normal to the normal. Are you clear on all this so far?

Then who is normal?

Many people who are not me would ask, "Am I normal?" to which most normal people would respond, "What, are you nuts?" which question we just dealt with in the paragraph above and which is probably a better question, and to which I would respond, "Probably, but then, who cares? Who wants to be normal anyway?" However, since we know there are lots of you out there worrying about being normal, we offer the following information as a public service.

The following public service information:

I think the best way to tell if you're normal is to examine your sense of humor. You would be considered a sick-o deviant by normal people, for example, if you were to laugh at any of the following scenarios, unless, of course, you were only laughing to impress abnormal sick and deviant people who are hanging out with you at the time. In that case, you might still have a chance to be normal.

'NORMAL' TEST

Would you laugh if:

1. While giving a speech to the nation, the chairman of the Federal Reserve picks up a glass to wet his parched lips and with the entire nation gasping in horror, takes a big slurp, and chokes on his false teeth which had been left soaking in his glass of water?

YES ☐   NO ☐

2. Former Attorney General and personal free legal service to former President Clinton, Janet Reno, during her campaign for the U.S. Senate, comes bounding onto the stage while shooting a campaign rock video with a 20 foot ribbon of toilet paper tucked into her leather hot pants and trailing along behind her?

YES ☐   NO ☐

3. Your neighbor kids rub hair-removal product all over their cat, Muffy, while Mom is gone?

YES ☐   NO ☐

4. Ralph Nadar reportedly falls asleep at the wheel smashing his S.U.V. into a 200-year-old, old growth Douglas fir tree injuring all 7 Oregon residents who are living inside or otherwise attached?

YES □   NO □

5. Your macho husband lies on the floor because while he's talking on the phone, your 2-year-old daughter toddles up and whacks him pretty hard as high as she can reach, to get his attention?

YES □   NO □

If you laughed at any of these, you would probably be considered by normal people to be on the fringes of the deviant range on the abnormal spectrum. On the other hand, you might be considered safely within the normal range for the politically incorrect, the twisted, and the sick and demented, who, incidentally, consider normal people humor disadvantaged or even neurotic.

2 How to tell if you are too smart

O.K. what if your problem has nothing to do with the confusion described above? If you asked, "Could my problem be that I'm so intelligent nobody else understands me?" What then?

I would respond with an enthusiastic, "Maybe." But consider that many who assume their problems are a function of their brilliance are, in reality suffering from a recently identified debilitating medical condition. What they have is known around mental health professionals, nut houses, and my office by its technical name: "Wildly Eccentric Individuals, Or the Danged Obnoxious." (WEIRDO is the acronym). So, if you've spent the last few years telling everybody you meet that other people don't understand you because you're so brilliant, it could very well be that you are simply a WEIRDO who has not yet been diagnosed. But, just to cover all the bases, we have written this chapter on really smart people, and since somebody obviously invented the TV remote, there must be at least a few people out there who really ARE brilliant and eccentric. In case you are one who suspects you might be among the brilliantly absent minded, we provide this test:

A test to determine if the reason people avoid you is because you are so smart you make them nervous

Section 1: Essay

Instructions: Read each question carefully. Answer each question on a sheet of lined paper or a napkin. You have 10 minutes. Begin now.

1. In minute detail, chronicle the history of Eastern philosophical thought from the beginning of the Bronze Age to the present. Be sure to consider the practical application of such thinking within regional social and religious constraints and it's eventual influence on the animated film and country music industries.

2. Using abstract language characters you have invented, explain calculus. (No electronic calculators allowed.)

3. Discover cold fusion. Describe in detail the economic benefits that will accrue to hunter-gatherer societies within the Amazon Basin as a result of your

invention giving special attention to atmospheric environmental models.

4. In twenty-five words or less elaborate the tenants of all major Zoroastrian religions of the ancient world.

5. Using chemicals found around your house, create an inexpensive antidote for each of the following: Anthrax, E Bola, Herpes, Gout, Environmental Extremism, and Breast Cancer. Then describe an effective, but inexpensive method of distribution of these medications, which will facilitate uninhibited free use of these antidotes in developing nations and Fresno.

6. Formulate a political strategy, which will culminate in world peace before the end of the current decade. Be prepared to defend the viability of your plans within the context of militant Islamic societies.

7. Invent a cure for old age.

8. Using chord combinations created entirely without outside influence, describe our solar system in music. Write your opus blending only the following instruments: A mandolin, a harmonica, a sitar, maracas, and a tuba.

9. You have been provided an electric toothbrush, a can opener, and a pair of cotton briefs. Using only these surgical tools, remove your occipital lobe. For liability purposes, be sure and follow generally accepted and sanitary surgical procedures.

10. Buy a professional sports franchise, operate it at a profit, and win a championship in a small market. Then, acting as athletic director of a school in a non-BCS conference, figure out a way to play for the national championship when your team has the best record in college football.

Section1 - EXTRA CREDIT:

Walk on water.

Section II. True/False

1. Have you ever had a real job?

"OK. I passed the test. So what can I do if I'm just so danged smart nobody understands me?"

This can be a real problem. What can you do?

In order to get a handle on this problem, you will need to imagine you're seeing the world through the eyes of all the little, common Forrest Gumps out there, those people who talk about you behind your back and hate you because they fear you. Imagine just for a moment that instead of a human intellectual prodigy, you were a worm or grub. Think for a minute. In this hypothetical case, what would be your main worries in life?

Believe it or not, this really isn't that far-fetched. Your more ancient body parts like your appendix remember back to the time when you were a simpler organism, when everything else in your world was trying to eat you. In those days, your biggest concern was, "Is today the day I get eaten by a tera-woodpecker-dactl" or "Where can I hide from this trilobite?" To keep from being a prehistoric Pop Tart, you had no choice but to either spend your life in hiding or convince all the hungry creatures you were either harmless or that you taste nasty. You could never allow them to know for one moment the truth, which was that you have a reasonable amount of intelligence, and, given the opportunity, you would eat THEM.

"OK, so, making this awkward, bogus comparison, in today's world, how does one symbolically avoid being eaten by all the virtual woodpeckers that surround us every day? How does one appear harmless to urban trilobites who fear them and want to eat them?" you ask. The obvious answer is that you try to blend in, and the best way to blend in is to act normal. Now can you see how important this concept of normal becomes?

A list of 13 simple things anyone can do to make people think he / she / it is normal no matter how strange he / she / it is

If you are having trouble with my slug, trilobite, and woodpecker illustration, if you are somebody who is so intelligent you don't relate to normal people, or if you are still struggling with this concept of normal for whatever reason, here are some things you can do which, we are told, common, every day, garden variety "normal people," do regularly to keep from being eaten (figuratively):

1. Stand in line for days to get the first tickets to whatever is the latest blockbuster motion picture, which everyone knows will be out in a few weeks on video and which you can easily then rent for a lot less money.

2. Whine incessantly about your job all the while wondering, if you didn't have this job, who else would be dumb enough to pay you to recover from your weekends.

3. Each year buy the latest book on the hottest fad diet and try it until you realize it will kill you or that it requires enormous effort and monumental life-changes.

4. Buy lots and lots of lottery tickets.

5. Read the supermarket tabloids and act as though you believe everything they say.

6. Pretend to care what all the stars and famous personalities are doing in their messed up personal lives, and pretend to jump on the bandwagon of all their misguided moral crusades.

7. Spend 5 or 6 hours each day watching mindless TV.

8. Watch professional wrestling and other artificial, over-hyped events. Even practice trash talking and work on some of your own moves.

9. Lecture your kids daily about how much you benefitted from working 37 hour days digging turnips on your hands and knees in 150 degree heat using a spade made of sandstone and being glad to have the opportunity.

10. Talk regularly to your cats using your baby voice normally reserved for infant humans.

11. Daydream about skimboarding at the beach during your parent's daily lecture about a 150 pound turnip digging for 37 hours in the sandstone.

12. Talk regularly to your babies in your cute voice usually reserved for pets.

13. Show ultimate support for the animal rights movement by wearing t-shirts and bumper stickers while you donate your apartment to be used as a sanctuary for wild roaches after your reduce the human population by feeding yourself to a malnourished hippo.

3 How to make people think you're normal

This book is breaking new wind, ...er, ground. For the first time in history, someone (me) is attempting to pass judgment on every conceivable human behavior and tell you what to do in absolutely any situation you could ever encounter. To the layman, especially one concerned with accuracy and truth, this appears to be an enormous, even impossible task. And that's not the only problem either. While criticizing behavior in this way is a common, every day responsibility for most garden-variety females, it is completely unnatural for a normal male; hence, as a guy, I realize I am taking on some huge risks, which will undoubtedly doom this project to failure and get me ostracized by my peers. But, since I know that a person who wants to launch big ships must do it in deep water, sometimes without

Donald Duck water wings, waders, or even a change of dry underwear while standing knee-deep in muck, and since many forms of failure could be considered an actual improvement over my current life, I figure, I must forge ahead in the name of science. So, here goes:

A comprehensive list of behaviors that would be considered abnormal to a normal person

Whenever watching TV:

Abnormal: Laughing at the lame jokes.

Normal: Committing violent and illegal acts inspired by the shows you watch; gagging; throwing up; sleeping; becoming more violent; whacking your children, husband, or sibling; committing more violent acts; robbing banks; trying a new copycat crime just for fun; grousing about the gratuitous sex and violence; grousing that there's not enough gratuitous sex and violence as you commit a violent, degrading, and illegal act; committing even more demented violent acts; and endlessly surfing channels pathetically hoping to find at least one show that doesn't insult your intelligence.

After sneezing:

Atypical: Wiping it on the person next to you, or

playing with it until it hardens and then rolling it into cool figures and little balls.

Typical: First, donning plastic gloves to protect you from coming into contact with potentially deadly bodily fluids, then using a handkerchief to clean up the mess; and, finally, putting the handkerchief back into your purse or pocket to be used again later.

While at the opera:

Abnormal: Gargling your Perier water, firing your gun into the air to get things moving, starting the wave, throwing your empty beer cans into the orchestra pit while yelling obscenities at the opposing players, who are known in the opera as villains.

Normal: Singing passionately and loudly along with the performers, making up your own harmony. (If your Italian is weak, it's OK to do this in English.)

Whenever you're served food you don't like:

Bad: Spitting it onto the hostess or gagging loudly and proclaiming you're being poisoned.

Good: While no one else is watching, dumping it into the pot of a nearby plant, or placing the food onto the plate of the person sitting next to you while he/she isn't looking.

When golfing:

Abnormal: Constantly giving helpful suggestions to other golfers in an effort to help them improve their scores.

Normal: Wrapping your putter around a tree and then, in order to take your mind off how badly you're playing, shooting some ducks and squirrels so you can take them home for food while undergoing a test to determine whether or not your cart is amphibious.

When throwing-up in public:

Wrong: Stirring around in it trying to pick out the big pieces.

Right: Being sure to dump out your shoes before you put them back on.

While losing at basketball:

Abnormal: Playing by the rules, showing good sportsmanship, and applauding honest effort even by the opposing team.

Normal: Whining incessantly and blaming the officials, opposing players, sun spots, Zeus, or the Pope for every shot you miss.

Whenever your obnoxious cat, Fluffy, or your silly, rat-like dog, Poopsie, gets flattened by a garbage truck:

Abnormal: Describing in graphic detail all the cute, little mannerisms she used to have to people who don't care.

Normal: Doing something useful with the material left over such as feeding it to Gus, your piranha, or using its carcass as a dust-rag.

After falling into a sewer or mud puddle:

Odd: Collecting samples so you can analyze them when you get back to the lab.

Less odd: Doing the backstroke, swimming laps, or splashing other people as they pass by and in every way pretending you are there because that's where you want to be and you're having a great time.

Whenever dieting:

Less Normal: After having eaten a celery stick, putting your finger down your throat, whacking yourself with a baseball bat, or stapling your ears to the fence to help you deal with the guilt and as a reminder to never do it again.

More Normal: Being pretty good about eating healthy things most of the time, but, once-a-day or so pulling a Twinkie out of your shoe and a Reeses Peanut Butter Cup from under the sofa. Taste-testing a few sample cookies you had hidden on top of the fridge, and just to control your cravings 'til dinner, snacking on a Twix, and munching a bag of potato chips.

While flying in an airplane:

Bad: Throwing up all over the other passengers, screaming "We're all going to die!" for the entire 3-hour flight, or sharing your latest lame joke or your most intimate secrets with the total stranger sitting next to you who doesn't care.

Good: Taking a double dose of sleeping pills to give you dreams of tropical paradise instead of worrying for the whole flight whether or not you'll get down alive.

When driving behind someone talking on a cellphone:

Wrong: Running them off the road into a tree.

Right: Keeping your distance so you can watch them run other drivers off the road into trees.

When going to the bank to make a withdrawal:

Abnormal: Handing the teller a note and then making everyone in the bank go into the vault and lie down while you empty the vault and all the cash drawers of any valuables.

Normal: Hoping those checks you wrote a day or two ago still haven't cleared, so there will still be enough money so the teller will give you what you need instead of embarrassing you in front of the other bank customers by loudly discussing your overdraft.

While driving behind a slow driver:

Not O.K.: Pulling your shotgun out from under the seat and shooting out his back window to send him a message.

O.K.: Visualizing yourself pulling your shotgun out from under the seat and shooting out his back window to send him a message.

4 Things normal people usually don't do

If you are regularly doing any of the following, you should stop now. These behaviors will not convince people you're normal:

> *-Chaining flocks of chickens to your nose ring.*

> *-Asking the airport security people to hold your grenade while you empty your pockets.*

> *-Going to work at your bank wearing nothing but a diaper and a Burger King crown.*

-Serving sautéed salamanders at
a formal dinner.

-Driving to work during rush hour on the
freeway riding a tricycle.

-Accepting a job as a salad.

-Accepting a job as a cheeseburger.

-Accepting a job as a speed bump.

-Accepting a job as a basketball referee.

-Sitting down in the lunchroom and chowing
down on your neighbor's foot.

-Sitting down in the lunchroom and
munching on a sack of marbles.

-Accepting a job as a toilet paper recycling specialist.

-Sitting down in the lunchroom and chowing down on a sack of 10-10-30-fertilizer.

-Tying your bag of golf clubs to the bumper of your car, making them ride outside as punishment for playing poorly.

-Gargling with Drain-O.

-Test-driving a chicken.

-Wrapping the water skiing rope around your neck a couple of times so it doesn't get away while you're skiing.

-Using your forehead to break chunks out of the driveway.

-Using your friend's forehead to break chunks out of the driveway.

-Having conversations with a rock.

-Having an argument with yourself that comes to blows.

-Having conversations with the rats and roaches in your apartment.

-Having conversations with your imaginary weasel friend, Ernie.

-Having violent arguments with the voices in your head.

-Taking your hamster out of the cage so you can blow your nose on it.

-Blowing your nose on your boyfriend's collar.

-Dining on the flowers in front of
your house.

-Selling your riding lawnmower because you
now plan to maintain your lawn by doing
your own grazing.

-Smoking black powder.

-Fighting Sparky for his Kibbles and Bits.

-Holding still and lying quietly while
your friend makes lizard tattoos on the
bottoms of your feet without
anesthetic.

-Tying your dog up to a strange truck.

-Sharing your parakeet with a python.

-Recycling your lame ideas.

-Recycling your boyfriends.

-Using a chain saw to scratch your back.

-Using a chain saw to scratch your friend's back.

-Body surfing down an elevator shaft.

-Good idea: Tying your cat to a strange truck.

-Kissing a gorilla.

> **-Diving in front of a speeding Semi truck to rescue a confused raccoon.**

There. That about covers it. If we have inadvertently omitted any abnormal behaviors, we are not responsible. In fact, we are pretty much completely (irresponsible). Also, this list may be culturally biased in favor of the abnormal.

5 A partial list of abnormal people

(for comparison purposes)

I live in a strange place. As near as I can tell, there are absolutely no normal people around me. Oh sure, I've met people from time to time who seem to be somewhat normal at first glance, but sure enough, once I got to know them a little better, they turned out to be as weird as a seagull's diet during the county fair.

Since I know many of my readers are worrying about being normal, to give them a point of reference, I am going to begin a partial list of the abnormal people I know so they can compare themselves. Also, in order to place everyone on an equal footing, we need to work toward getting all of these abnormal people some kind of government entitlement to compensate for being a strange as a defense lawyer's explanation for a serial killer's dynamite collection.

Abnormal descriptions

First, I would probably consider my wife, Robyn, normal if it weren't for her bad eyesight, below normal driving skills, and the fact that she's abnormally attractive. Steve, too, is close to the normal range in most areas, but then he's overweight and vertically challenged. Stan has the opposite problem; the characteristics keeping him abnormal are his underweight brought on by an abnormally high metabolism along with being humor disadvantaged. Forrest is normal in most ways you wouldn't notice; he's normal except for being a racial minority working in a non-traditional, abnormal occupation surrounded by a bunch of weird-os. Erin is normal in almost every way, except she would probably be considered abnormally smart, and yet, ironically, she spells all her words phonetically which is abnormal given the fact that our entire language is spelled abnormally. Jason is above the normal range height-wise, and below normal in luck with wrecking cars and, therefore, has abnormal insurance premiums. The other Jason is normal in size, except for his short legs and has below normal eyesight and abnormal tolerance for obnoxious people. No one has ever considered Drew normal, but everyone still likes him, which is not his object in life anyway, which is clearly not normal, but which is definitely healthy; and he would rather pass than shoot, which is abnormal even for most point guards. Rick gets less than normal sleep, and is therefore abnormally socially inhibited for which he tries to compensate by telling abnormal jokes. Deb hasn't been perfectly normal ever since she had her thyroid removed, and of course, Bob can't be normal because he's Irish and has been married to Deb for over 25 years, which can't be normal. Lamar has abnormal memory skills, which gives him an unfair advantage at chess, but, unfortunately, he drives erratically, which outside of California is considered not normal. Kelsey has abnormally beautiful hair, but she sunburns abnormally even in the shade. Cameron would be pretty normal except he eats his cereal without milk and then drinks 2-gallons-a-day in a glass. And, of course, Dana is normal, except she talks to herself abnormally, is always cold and can do math.

Unfortunately, we don't have space here for descriptions of all the people I know who are abnormal and why. Therefore, we will just have to be content to list the names of the abnormal people. Feel free to use any reasons you want for considering these people abnormal.

A partial list of abnormal people for comparison purposes

The following people are not normal:

> Burt, Randy, Lesa, Dave, LaRene,
> Ray, Drew, Cathy, Danny, Carolyn,
> Vikki, Wiley, Brock, John, Christine,
> Kelsey, Ellis, Jade, Jesse, Justin,
> Brian, Brian, Brian, Brian, Nila, Lisa,
> Jeff, Cameron, Kimberly, Jamie,
> Brandon, Charlie, Evan, Jeannie,
> Joseph, Kelci, C.J., Hunter, Hayden,
> Cassie, Rebecca, Megan, Richard,
> Al, Mildred, Kerrie, Scott, Karl,
> Chelsae, Brad, Tyler, Trent, Kendall,
> Brigham, Chriss, Jerry, Rebecca,
> Ryan, John, Jon, Todd, Mary, Heather,
> Amy, Brock, Michael, Ted, Jean, Val,
> Giselle, Erin, Kolton, Jed, Taylor,
> Vikki, Karl, Mckenzie, Bracken, Sara,
> Courtney, and Grandpa.

If you did not find your name on this list, please don't be offended; that would be abnormal.

A useful bunch of information having nothing to do with the topic of this book inserted here to give you a break from the rigors of trying to comprehend normal

Making Telemarketers Pay

Remember the last time you just sat down in the middle of an important telephone call and you got beeped indicating another call was coming in, so you interrupted your very important call to find on the other end of the line a telemarketer with a terrific deal? Or, remember the other day, you had been working hard, up all night, and you were just getting to sleep a little early because of an important appointment early the next morning when you heard the phone ring and, "Hello is this Mr. Alfred?" (Because of the odd foreign accent and the mispronunciation of your name, you begin to suspect that a telemarketer has invaded your space.)

Because this is such an annoyance, many people have had the old "we do not accept solicitations" recording attached to their phone line. What a shame. You can have so much fun and recreation with telemarketers.

Try the following ways of enjoying your telemarketers:

1. With no explanation, just begin to talk like Donald Duck.

2. Scream, "Hello! Is this 911? My baby's choking! What do I do?"

3. Interrupt her and begin to describe your hernia operation in graphic detail.

4. While he is talking say, "Hello, hello. Melvin! The phone has crashed again!"

5. Don't say a word; just breath heavily.

6. Make cool airplane or truck sounds.

7. Say, "Stop! Before you say another word, kiss your phone receiver. I love you! You can run to the farthest corner of the world and I will still find you."

8. Ask her specific questions about members of her family and then threaten to start killing people if they don't leave you alone.

9. Scream or whistle as loud as you can into the phone and then, using your announcer's voice say, "This has been a test of the emergency

broadcasting system. This is only a test."

10. Say, "I thought you were the kidnappers. If they call while I'm talking to you we'll miss them and they'll kill Bonnie. Oh No! I hear the beep!"

11. Instead of saying anything, scratch your fingernails on the blackboard.

12. Have an accomplice in the background say, "If you can keep him talking for just another 30 seconds, we can fix his location and get a swat team in there."

13. Say, "Here, let me call you back on your home phone later tonight when I have time to talk. What's your number?"

6 A Study In Normal Contrast

Here is another opportunity for you to see how you, personally, measure up on the old normal scale. Compare your life with the examples below.

Pets

Normal pets: a dog, a bird, a parakeet, a hamster, a guppy, a politician, a rabbit, a goat, a horse, a python, a newspaper reporter, a roach, a frog, a professional athlete, a tyrannical foreign leader needing money and empathy from the American left wing.

Abnormal pets: a cat, a skunk, a rock, a rhino, an alien, a chainsaw, a barracuda, a triceratops, a rabid bat, a rabid bear, Fred, a rabid boyfriend, a crocodile, your wart, anthrax spores, an intern, Frankenstein.

Transportation:

Normal Transportation: your feet, a car, a bicycle, a bus, a wild imagination, a train, a rickshaw, an airplane, a horse, a spaceship, skis, a skateboard.

Abnormal Transportation: a broom, a carpet, a cow, a buzzard, Spam, a lizard, an intercontinental ballistic missile, your face, a spoon, a golf tee, a wild boar, an angry shark, a sand dollar, pudding.

Dreams:

Normal Dreams: Cruising around town in a chauffeur-driven limo; sinking the winning shot at the buzzer in the championship game; lean, muscular, good-looking guys doing your housework; Peter Pan; being president of the world; life as a super hero.

Abnormal Dreams: Falling from a 100-story building and hitting the ground before you wake up, being a bus-boy at Denny's, hijacking an airplane, having to go and then feeling sudden relief, having no dreams at all, being a sea cucumber, lying in an ant bed with whipped cream and caramel all over your body while dining on a rubber boot, imagining airplanes blowing up.

Dessert:

Normal Desserts: apple pie, ice cream, anything chocolate , lemon meringue pie, fresh trout cooked on an open fire, a Krispy Kreme Donut, a banana split, a big pile of whipped cream.

Abnormal Desserts: a gerbil, the knobs from your dashboard, antifreeze, a bottle of shampoo, Dog Food, your fingernails, your date's fingernails, your date's toenails, a blob of rancid pond scum, the banana peel, black powder, a roll of paper towels, the governor.

Thoughts & Feelings:

Normal thoughts/feelings: sadness for mankind's inhumanity to man, gratitude for everything your mom has done for you, love for your neighbor, contempt for the bad drivers on the road, serenity, joy to be alive, wonder about your dog being dead, nausea from listening to political infomercials, confusion about why your car won't start, anger over poor long distance service, concern about wretched media, disgust for unprincipled, short sighted politicians.

Abnormal Thoughts and Feelings: love for your hand grenade, desire to bite the head off a duck, gratitude for your jailer, belief that everybody thinks you're funny, trust in your politicians, worry you might be happier as a trout, lust for Madeline Albright, desire to stretch a worm until it breaks, the need to poke your friend's finger up your nose, depression over the declining skunk population, affection for your warts, certainty that your country or state can't function without your leadership, passion for Brussels sprouts, joy over having successfully completed terrorist school.

Recreation:

Normal Recreation: golf, basketball, whining about old sports injuries, softball, exaggerating your accomplishments, pitching insults, movies, camping in bad weather, whining about politics, skiing, playing chess, whining about taxes, painting, whining about the weather, boating, whining about poor service.

Abnormal Recreation: torturing small animals, watching daytime TV, planning to blow up The White House, contemplating your navel, playing practical jokes on the US Marines, getting tattoos on your eyelids, collecting belly button lint, listening to rap music, whining about having too much money, collecting deadly bacteria, crank-calling the Pentagon.

Phobias:

Normal Phobias: fear of heights (agriphobia), fear of water (aquaphobia), fear of mean dogs (fidophobia), fear you can't pay your taxes (lien-o-phobia), fear you left someone off the guest list (ostracize-o-phobia), fear your fly is open (flashphobia), fear your children will marry a celebrity (sued-o-phobia), fear of having a visit from an obnoxious person who won't leave (pest-o-phobia).

Abnormal Phobias: fear of being too healthy ('buff-o-chondria), fear of being competent (mechanicophobia), fear of being murdered by your spouse (O.J.phobia) , fear of wearing deodorant (reek-a-phobia), fear of having the F.B.I. find out you're planning a terrorist attack on a local mink farm during ground hog day (rodentolibrophobia), fear of being married to an attractive person (whoa-o-phobia) .

Faux Pas:

Normal Faux Pas: wearing plaid pants with a striped shirt, serving red wine with saur kraut and refried beans, driving a mini-van, wearing anything I pick out, asking a chubby woman who isn't pregnant when she's due, misusing a big word.

Abnormal Faux Pas: lighting the fuse to the dynamite in a room filled with gasoline fumes; wearing a tuxedo and tails with major spaghetti stains; making a recording for your answering machine which is supposed to be funny but isn't; cutting me off in traffic because you're distracted and talking on your cell phone; cutting down a giant redwood tree to block the road so the loggers can't get to the redwood;

Diseases:

Normal Diseases: Gout, chronic bronchitis, Strep throat, hemorrhoids, schizophrenia, leprosy, toenail fungus, mumps, adolescent psychosis, Hodgkin's disease, Lou Gherig's disease, halitosis, the flu, brain flatulence.

Abnormal Diseases: terminal stupidity, chronic obnoxious syndrome, terrorism, adolescence, chronic cranial obesity (Howard Sterns Disease), humor impairment.

Normal vs. Abnormal

Normal Abnormalities: Poor memory, bad eyesight, small cranium, large cranium, extraordinarily rapid facial hair growth, genius, marmoset ears.

Abnormal Abnormalities: having a benign growth on your face which looks like a face, having a total absence of internal organs, being a genius only in figuring out creative ways to use duct tape, being a prodigy in your ability to become fatigued.

Clues About Cracking Up

Don't get all smug now just because you've always thought you were normal in the past. The truth is, most people out there who are looney don't know they're crazy because they're nuts. That's the problem. So, even if you have always considered yourself normal, everybody else could already have been observing your slide into insanity and have you pegged as a wack-o and you, in your looniness are simply oblivious. Here are a few clues to tell you that you might finally be cracking up.

1. The apartment next door is complaining because the constant banging of your head on the wall keeps them up all night.

2. The conversations you have with yourself lately have begun to erupt into violent confrontations.

3. You have reached the point where your nose is so full that you can fit no more beans up there, so now you are beginning to poke them up the noses of complete strangers.

4. You have become a well-recognized celebrity, and now you are beginning to champion politically correct causes.

5. Each morning after donning your loincloth you run through the mall yelling unintelligible gibberish.

6. You and a few of your buddies have decided you are now ready to take on the U.S. Marines.

7. You want to go to law school.

8. You have decided you would like to try making a living as a humor writer.

9. You are more concerned about the deaths of turkeys, lab rats, and cute animals than you are the deaths and suffering of human beings.

10. You have begun to look forward with enthusiasm to your daily flogging.

7 Abnormal drivers

*You can seem normal even if you're a clueless wiener-head behind the wheel

We have noticed an all-too-common and interesting phenomenon occurring regularly in our society. Some people who seem perfectly sane when taking out the trash, dialing 911, starting a riot, or poisoning gophers, become vacuum-brained weasels when allowed behind the wheel of a car. Whenever this transformation occurs, the experience usually looks something like this: Let's say you are driving along on a two-lane highway going a safe, comfortable, and very nearly legal speed, when you come up behind some loser who is cruising at 15 MPH below the already insulting officially posted speed recommendation. You are then stuck plodding behind him doing your best snail imitation. This wouldn't be such a big deal except that today your wife's labor pains are only 90 seconds apart and she is about to deliver twins. As your luck would have it, for 30 agonizing minutes, every time the yellow passing line is in your lane, there is a semi coming the other way.

After frantically following this rutabaga-brain for a couple of hours while he chats with another passenger, oblivious to the fact that the line of frustrated motorists held back by his napping turtle speed is now bumper to bumper and extends through three time zones, miracle of miracles, you finally have a chance to pass. The clouds part, the sun shines through, the line is in the other lane, and there is no semi in view from the opposite direction. You signal left, push the pedal to the metal and move into the passing lane with retrorocket flames roaring out your tailpipe. Relief is in sight.

As you come up alongside the slow-moving driver, you have to sneak a peek, because you can't remember ever having seen the offspring of vegetable pulp. As you move to pass him, he suddenly notices he is being passed. He gets an alarmed look on his face as it finally registers in his tiny brain that for the past few hours, he has been inconveniencing half the population of the Western U.S. Panic is in his eyes as he glances in his rear-view mirror and witnesses this endless parking lot crawling along behind him. Gasping in embarrassment and horror as the enormity of this faux pas registers in his microscopic gray matter, his competitive reflexes take over. He stomps on the gas and begins to accelerate. Ironically, he is finally going at a pretty good speed. Unfortunately, you are still in the passing lane facing oncoming traffic, and now he seems to be racing you!

Since you aren't ready to explode in a ball of flames from a head-on crash, you strain to coax a little more horse power from your shuddering sedan, but the delay has made it impossible for you to complete your attempt to pass before another semi, now barreling toward you in the passing lane, would meet you head-on. You have no choice but to brake with all your might and slide back behind this hemorrhoid of the highway until another passing opportunity comes along, which could be days.

Meanwhile, now, with no cars in front or to the side, to distract him, his companion begins a new, very animated, and jolly conversation. Old Cauliflower Cranium relaxes and resumes driving at less than half the speed limit, once again oblivious to the growing queue of motorists behind him who's anger is being diffused by fists pounding on dash boards and teeth gnawing on steering wheels. If, just for a second, he could hear the sounds outside his window, he would hear the cries of lovely, newborn twins bouncing along in the front seat of your car.

If you are reading this book and happen to be a judgment-impaired brain allergy who regularly drives on my roads at half the speed limit (and let's be honest, there are millions of you out there who do), if you want to live to a normal old age, you have only 2 options: #1 Turn over all driving in the future to a sane, competent designated driver or #2: Suicide. Whatever you do, **do not reproduce!**

8 More things normal people usually don't do

Here are a few more things we forgot to tell you not to do if you want to seem normal:

> *-Try to get up enough speed to drive your motor scooter through a big rock.*

> *-Use explosives to weed your garden.*

> *-Shave your llamas.*

-Put your saddle on the bottom
side of your horse.

-Throw rocks at your own car.

-Brush your teeth with Liquid Plumber.

-Pretend your JELL-O is a cell phone.

-Use firecrackers to clean your ears.

-Float over Niagara Falls in a kitty litter box.

-Float over Niagara Falls on a Zucchini.

-Float over Niagara Falls on a
heat-seeking missile.

-Perform surgery on yourself to re-design
your nose making it seven feet long.

-Clean your car with a flamethrower.

-Pour Anthrax on your cornflakes.

-Name your children after terminal diseases.

-Use a duck for a catcher's mitt.

-Spread gravel on your sandwich.

-Give yourself a tattoo using a spot welder.

-Try to cure your hiccoughs by spending an
hour in the washing machine on spin cycle.

-Bath your dog in liquid drain cleaner.

-Hang your hammock on high voltage wires.

-Stick your tongue into the toaster.

-Spend the Christmas holidays shopping in the Gobi Desert.

-Use spun glass insulation for your mattress.

-Jump out of an airplane using a parachute made from wet Kleenex tissue.

-Jump out of an airplane with a salami for a parachute.

-Pick a fight with a wolverine over a piece of beef jerky.

-Hunt wild boar with a BB gun.

-Use battery acid to unclog your sinuses.

-Wear your underwear on the outside of your clothes.

-Make jokes about bombs with airport security personnel.

-Make obscene, crank phone calls on your picture phone.

-Throw snowballs at black limousines.

-Try to play Frisby by spinning weasels around the park.

-Mail yourself to Afghanistan in a small box filled only with yourself and Styrofoam peanuts.

-Go everywhere with your shoes on upside down.

-Jump off a tall building with only a spaghetti noodle for a bunji chord and no helmet.

-Wear a dead possum around your neck.

-Open your house to all the little orphaned snakes, rats, and roaches in your part of the country.

-Allow yourself to be used as fish bait.

-Crawl on your belly over hot coals.

-Lie ~~on~~ your back on hot coals.

-Chow down on hot coals.

-Chow down on broken glass.

-Snort Cayenne peppers.

-Let Count Dracula give you a big smooch.

-Relax for lunch on the railroad tracks.

-Let your older brother try to shoot an apple off your head with his rocket launcher.

-Marry an insect.

-Marry someone just to cheer her up because she's miserable.

-Grow the hair in your nose fifteen feet long and give it a perm.

9 Normal corporate philosophies

A few years ago, a whole cluster of books came out touting the value of a corporate philosophy. From these philosophies sprang numerous slogans and company mottos. Now days, every normal company, large and small, has a corporate philosophy. Some are published; some are not. Some are well known; some are obscure. Some would surprise you.

Here at Apricot Press, we try to be trendy too. We also want to seem normal, and to have a realistic shot at paying some of our bills. So, we spent a few days wrangling, trying to decide on a corporate slogan that everyone could "buy into." I personally argued for a big sounding corporate slogan, one that would make people think we were mighty and powerful, which conveyed an image of cutting edge thinking and sound business sense, and which would help us qualify for a corporate American Express card.

Unfortunately, my wife, Robyn, was way too honest and principled for that. So, after hours and hours of arguing, we wound up with the following slogans, which I personally disapproved of because they were way too accurate to be of much value in our marketing efforts:

Apricot Press: "We understand how hard it is to keep your facts straight."

Apricot Press: "It makes us uncomfortable when people yell at us."

Apricot Press: "Maybe you won't be offended."

Apricot Press: "When you care enough to give the best, but maybe they don't deserve it."

Apricot Press: "When you care enough to give the best, but they would have no idea how much you spent."

Apricot Press: "When you care enough to give the best, but they probably wouldn't even know what it was."

Apricot Press: "When you care enough to give the best, but you would most likely see it being used as a doorstop."

Apricot Press: "Good at words; bad at math."

Apricot Press: "Please buy our stuff so we can pay our bills."

We are not the only company in America who had to work pretty hard to come up with a viable company slogan. Thanks to a campaign of exhaustive industrial espionage, acting under false pretenses, we have acquired the private notes and deliberations of numerous companies. These deliberations produced a bundle of corporate philosophies, slogans, and mottos, which just might surprise you... or maybe not. Some of these first ones will be familiar.

Hallmark Cards: "When you care enough to send the very best."

Walmart: "Our people make the difference."

Chevrolet Motors: "Like a Rock"

Fred Meyer: "What's on your list today?

Budweiser: "King of beers"

Smith and Edwards: "We've got whatever you need - if we can find it"

I say that if I have to use an honest corporate slogan, everyone else should too. Corporate America should dust off some of some of the old slogans which were never approved, but which, in many cases are much more accurate than the ones they use now. Who knows, maybe even some other business out there could use them. In fact, if truth in advertising really was: "truth-in-advertising," all companies would most likely end up with slogans and philosophies like these. Take a look.

EXXON: "Constantly maneuvering to get a higher percentage of your paycheck."

KENTUCKY FRIED CHICKEN: "Proving once again that chicken doesn't necessarily have to be bland or good for you."

THE INTERNET: "Hoping some day to help a non-porn company turn a profit."

DISNEY: "Politically correct so you don't have to be."
        or
"Bet you won't let YOUR daughter wear skirts as short as ours!"

ABC NEWS: "Striving to be as sensational as the supermarket tabloids."

MCDONALDS: "Proving once again that great advertising beats bland food any day."

PLANNED PARENTHOOD: "Hey kids! You don't need parents; you've got us!"
        or

"Helping kids hide dangerous behavior from nosey parents-because it's good for business."

IRS: "We've upped our standards. Up yours."

WALMART: "Helping small local business owners change careers."
        or
"Our people put your people out of business."
        or
"Soon to be your only choice."

THE AIRLINES: "Hope the planes don't crash."

ANHEISER BUSCH: "Sure, we're working hard to encourage under age consumers not to use our products. Honest."

LOS ANGELES LAKERS: "We may be spoiled, arrogant, and immature, but we make millions."

THE NATIONAL EDUCATION ASSOCIATION:
"Controlling minds, controlling money."

THE UNITED WAY: "Believe it or not, less efficient than the federal government."
        or
"Where your generosity supports our bureaucracy."
        or
"If you look close enough, you may find ONE of our charitable causes you feel O.K. supporting."

VISA/MASTER CARD: "Hey, Cool! We get a cut of everything you buy!"

GREEN PEACE: "There's gold in peoples' phobias!"
> or

"Consolidating our power to control your world."
> or

"Tying up the courts for decades to make the world safe from opposing opinions."

THE FEDERAL GOVERNMENT: "Ever growing until we are you."

COORS: "20,000-adolescent traffic fatalities-a-year certainly couldn't be our fault."

HOLLYWOOD: "We think you just can't watch enough sex."

EPA: "We want to control your property."

ABERCROMBIE AND FITCH: "The more we charge, the more you want us."
> or

"Where snooty customers provide free advertising."

THE NATIONAL GUARD: "Let us impose ourselves into the middle of your 2000-year-old incomprehensible ethnic squabble."

DEMOCRATIC PARTY: "Whatever is wrong in your life, don't worry, the government will fix it. Here's your money. Vote for us."

REPUBLICAN PARTY: "Government is too big and intrusive. Here's your money. Vote for us."

HYUNDAI MOTORS: "Quality is overrated."

ATT: "The reason we charged such exorbitant rates in the old days had nothing to do with the fact that we were a monopoly."
>   or
"We don't care. We don't have to."

The POWER COMPANY: "Trust us. Forcing us to compete won't bring your rates down."

The STATE GOVERNMENT: "Of course your property taxes went up again."

The NEW YORK YANKEES: "Raising ticket prices once more, so we can buy all the best players."

REYNOLDS TOBACCO: "Maybe you won't become a statistic."

CITIBANK: "Having a wonderful time with your money."

RALPH NADAR: "Everything will kill you."
>   or
"A little bit of freedom for you little people is way too much."
>   or
"Making millions in law suits as we lower everyone's standard of living."

The A.C.L.U. "Opposed to everything good-just to be fair."

Apricot Press: "When we can't pay our bills it makes us break out in hives."

We know that other small companies have struggled trying to come up with a good corporate motto or slogan. So, if you have a small business, you might try one of these:

"Our people are indifferent."

"Our employees earn minimum wage."

"We're confused."

A construction company: Guys like us make all of your bildingz."

Your local bank: "Limiting your returns to keep our costs down."

Auto repair shop: "There are actually some cars that will make the noise while we're listening."

Apricot Press: "Happily working to support 89 different government agencies."

Your business: "Currently paying payables in less than 9 months."

"You can make me fix it, but you can't make me like it."

"50 employees, all watching the clock."

"If I only had your piddly problem, you wouldn't hear me whining."

"Cutting costs, but not profits."

Apricot Press: "Often waiting only 116 days for our receivables."

More entertaining but unrelated stuff

13 Good reasons to watch TV

1. Your intelligence is in no danger of being insulted.

2. You don't get enough sleaze and sex in real life, magazines, and movies.

3. You want to see how every problem in the world can be solved in an hour or less (45 minutes if you include commercials).

4. You are struggling with the concept of politically correct, and so you need a way to be thoroughly instructed so you never make errors in your thinking.

5. You are sick and tired of having to do all your own thinking; you just want Hollywood tell you what to believe.

6. You're weary of depth. You want your life to be superficial, artificial and shallow.

7. You have had it with ugly people. You only want to look at young, thin, beautiful people.

8. You understand that your life is irrelevant. You

are ready to accept the fact that only the indolent rich have a meaningful existence. You agree with the notion that salt-of-the-earth hard working self-sacrificing family people of every kind live empty lives. Everything you do must be validated by Hollywood people because they can tell you how things are supposed to be.

9. You constantly need to be reminded to drink more beer.

10. You have finally grown to the point where all you want for news are exaggerated, emotional human-interest stories of no real significance. You don't mind waiting and watching for them because even trivial stuff is so much fun when it's sensationalized and exaggerated.

11. You only want to see one side of everything.

12. You thoroughly enjoy watching all adults portrayed as bumbling incompetents, narrow-minded bigots, and vicious predators, and you want your kids to grow up believing kids are competent, smart, and they don't need adults.

13. You feel it's about time religions and monogamous married people had their comeuppance. It's time they were portrayed in a more evil, narrow-minded light.

10 More or less normal

Do people who are weird know they are weird? This is a question with far reaching ethical considerations, which somebody else will hopefully be qualified to deal with.

Let's say for a moment that you know a person who wears polyester pants hiked up to his armpits, has a goofy haircut, uses masking tape to hold his glasses together, and watches Jerry Springer. Does he know he's a dork? Does he do this on purpose?

Do all the people who decorate their yards with fake little animals and gnomes know that these gargoyles and flamingoes are symbolically shouting to the normal people authorized to pass judgment that a gaggle of dorks live in this pen?

Do people who take fat cells from their buttock region and have them injected into their lips know that if people find out they did this all their relatives will move to the other side of the exercise yard and their former boy friends will smear antiseptic alcohol on their lips out of disgust from having contact with cells that grew to maturity on someone's posterior?

Being intrigued by these questions, I began scientific research to find out once and for all if people who are abnormal know it. On the radio I ran some ads and announced we needed volunteers for a study to find a cure for weirdness and I needed some goofballs to volunteer to be studied. OK, so maybe I didn't use those exact words, but doctors run similar ads wanting people to volunteer to have their hemorrhoids waxed. Which is worse?

The point is nobody responded to my ads, so we had no choice but to do our experiment on animals. Accordingly, we dressed Sparky up in flood pants, hiked his shorts up, and gave him a weird haircut and a temporary bubblegum tattoo on his forehead. (Animal rights lawyers take note: we violated no laws here.) Sparky didn't seem to like the research much, but he would hold still as long as we kept his bowl full so he could slurp his beef broth.

From this, we logically concluded that people with dog breath genuinely don't care if they look weird, but they prefer running around without any clothes on as long as their dish is full. We're working hard to find some scientific value in this particular information, but it was worth the effort just watching Sparky, and it's fun to ponder tough questions like: If people are weird and they know they're weird, doesn't it logically follow that the rest of us are justified in sticking them upside down in garbage cans, slamming them in lockers, or just generally abusing them unmercifully? Seems logical enough to me, because if they know they are weird and they ever got tired of the abuse, they could stop, unless they are under contract or something, which would pose an entirely different set of ethical questions. This gets us to the next question.

The Next Question

Is there anyone out there who really wants to be normal?

I teach classes at a local college, and in order to stay on the cutting edge of the latest research, I periodically do an experiment on some of my classes. I like using normal students as guinea pigs because it's so satisfying to get them all upset. For example, this past semester I made up an impossibly tough test on a bunch of material that we hadn't covered in class. (Yes, I know; my colleagues and I do this all the time.) But this time I had a reason besides laziness or stupidity. I was doing social research. When the students got their tests back, not surprisingly they all hollered like stuck pigs because they scored below 30%, which as many of you know can be considered a poor grade even at most feel good state colleges, and my students were all grumbling and whining while I laughed sardonically. Next, we began a discussion of where to set the grading curve in order to be fair. As most of you know fairness is treasured above all other virtues in our society today, above rightness, above accuracy, above strength, above truth, justice, and the American way, even above reality. So we were having this discussion about where to set the curve since the best of their scores were in the 30s. Then, in the middle of this discussion, I invited Roland to the front. We will call him Roland, since that's his name and since he had been very quiet throughout the discussion because he would have been mortified if anyone found out he had scored a 97 on my brutal test. Naturally, I exposed his accomplishment and then fawned all over Roland, congratulating him on doing such a good job. Meanwhile, the other students cursed and spat and described the barbaric rituals they were going to perform on him if they ever caught him alone. But, I knew they were only kidding.

Roland was clearly not normal. In spite of his nerdiness, except for the pocket protector, clothes that didn't match, and bad haircut, even without research, I knew that everyone in that class would have gladly traded places with Roland. This proves to me that deep down inside, most people really don't want to be normal, and that even if you are a rotten professor and you do a lousy job preparing your students for your tests and for life, odds are that some geek in the class will score high enough on the test to bail you out and make it look to your colleagues and the public as though kids these days are just slackers.

11 Normal opinions

Since I have declared myself the ultimate expert in the world, and final arbiter on what can be considered normal, I have begun to receive some criticism, unjustified as it is. Accordingly, I would like to state unequivocally that just because a person doesn't know anything about something, doesn't mean he can't have a strong opinion about it. Narrow-minded thinking like that could have a disastrous impact on our economy. For example, if people were expected to know any actual facts about political issues, many of the already pathetic 40% of registered voters would stay home leaving something like 1% still voting. The millions of deranged and lunatic fans who so vocally second-guess basketball coaches and officials might become uncomfortable with their second guessing and stop coming to games out of boredom. Not to mention, of course, the entire psychological profession would suddenly need a new job.

One subject on which I have strong opinions and virtually no reliable information is school teaching. Having taught for many years, I have very strong opinions as you can imagine. I have survived many years in the classroom because of the brilliant teaching strategy I developed and shared with many of my colleagues.

A brilliant teaching strategy

I found the key is to relax. You can't get all worked up about trying to get students to learn. They hate that. This can lead to anger, frustration, hives and twitches. Instead, go to work in areas where it's easier to make a difference; areas which will allow you to keep a low profile, to merge with the educational landscape, seem normal, and make no waves; areas which will transform you into a "normal" teacher. These important skills include: Speaking in a monotone voice, developing devious ways of writing trick questions on exams, creative ways of denying students sufficient time between classes to go to the bathroom, the ability of appearing intimidating to weak-minded students, a condescending and arrogant aura, and allowing your listening skills to atrophy through disuse.

One very important principal (No pun intended) you must internalize is that good teachers never allow themselves to be pinned down. Failing students are just going to blame you for their bad grades and claim you lost their work anyway. You might as well justify their suspicions. I discovered the simplest way of being evasive is to take the daily piles of student work that accumulate, and instead of grading it, take it to the shredder. Once you have done this, you are free to insert any numbers into the grade book you want. Then, instead of giving grades based upon merit, for example a "C" or "D" grade, which causes so much stress, a normal teacher can operate one-hundred percent on the suck-up system. He or she can give every student an "A" and even back it up with the numbers in the book. By using this grading method you will never have to deal with angry parents. You will greatly increase the child's self worth giving her a feeling of accomplishment for beating the system. And, best of all, you won't need to expend huge amounts of energy preparing to actually teach anything to the students. Teachers who give every kid an A get to sit around parent teacher conferences in an orgy of praise for the little Einsteins instead of grappling with how to help them learn something; and never have to deal with the angry parents of snotty little crying sniveling spoiled students crying favoritism.

A variation on this theme

If, instead of sliding through with as little effort and trouble as possible, your goal is to enhance your career, make money, or improve your position of power, you can apply a small twist to this proven technique. You can give "D" s and "F" s to students you don't like, or to parents you're not afraid of, and save the A's for the students you like, or from whom you need something, or who are in danger of threatening to poison your dog. Benefits of this approach include a heavenly classroom environment with no discipline problems, because all the kids will be walking on eggs knowing if you don't like them, they flunk. Other benefits include rapid career advancement, and spending all day around kids who will do pretty much anything you want because they know their grade depends entirely upon your whims. And normally, you will get some cool bribes. And remember: as an added bonus you get large chunks of leisure time because you aren't spending all your prep periods and evenings grading those lame little papers.

I developed this strategy after dozens of experiences like this: Let's say you are a teacher and you had a boy in your class who cheated. You knew he cheated. You had incontrovertible hard evidence he cheated. After confronting him with the evidence, the little weasel even admitted he cheated. An inexperienced teacher might be tempted to give him a "0" on this assignment, which would drop his slimy little grade from an A- to a "C" and call his parents. As soon as his mom finds out, she will throw a screaming fit because, being a mom she senses her child's pain from a school district away. And she also intuitively knows that anything bad that ever happens to her child must be due to planned unfairness and persecution. Of course she would schedule an appointment with me, the evil teacher. In the intervening time, men in black will get hold of this kid and erase his memory, because by the time Mom drags him in to straighten you out, he has completely forgotten his confession; he also forgot the evidence. After listening to his mom get herself all worked up, he has become quite certain that you intentionally failed to even give him the assignment because you have singled him out for nasty teacher persecution because you hate him and want him to fail.

After showing your incontrovertible evidence to his mom to justify consequences for his cheating, and listening to her call you a liar and listening to the principal and counselor pose a few dozen possible explanations and compromise solutions to this "dilemma," it would most likely occur to you that you're the only one in the building concerned with the kids education and character.

You're not stupid. You happily apologize for being such a jerk and change the kid's grade to an A. Then, to avoid any possibility of future similar misunderstandings, you quickly change everyone else's grade in the class to an A; otherwise, it wouldn't be fair.

After years of experiences like this, I figure if a parent will go to all the trouble of driving into the school and yelling at me, and coming up with all those creative explanations for her kid's rotten behavior, SHE deserves an A, and since I can't give HER an A, it's only fair to give it to her kid. What better way to prepare kids to get along in the real world?

13-Reasons why you, being a normal person, would leave corporate America for a career teaching school

1. You believe that owning new, fashionable clothes is a waste of money.

2. You don't mind working for 14 hours a day, while only getting paid for 6.

3. Young people today all show authority figures such great respect.

4. You don't mind being blamed for all of society's problems; after all, somebody's got to do it.

5. You want to bail out the lazy, incompetent, spineless, and disinterested parents by doing all the rotten jobs they don't want to while raising their kids for them.

6. If you didn't get them in school, you would normally just go home and put a dozen or so spit-wads in your hair anyway.

7. Every 2 or 3 years you feel this compelling desire to grovel and beg the unappreciative legislature for a 1.6% cost-of-living raise.

8. You enjoy doing thousands of kind things for people who don't notice, and who don't appreciate them.

9. When you finally cash in your chips, you want to go out with your boots on in a blaze of gunfire from the automatic weapon of an angry 15-year-old with an attitude.

11. You just can't get enough of your own kids, so you feel you need to raise other peoples' children too.

12. June

13. July

14. August

12 Questions & Answers

FROM THE ULTIMATE, OMNISCIENT ARBITER OF NORMALNESS

Richard Weinerman from El Borracho, New Mexico writes:

Hey, Yo Judge: It seems that every morning when I get dressed, I forget something. Two-days ago, I forgot my socks. Yesterday, I forgot to put on my aftershave. This morning I came to work in my shorts. Is this normal?

Dear Mr. Weinerman: My question is: "what kind of imbecile would be sitting around wondering if this is normal?" And the answer is, "Probably the kind of people who would also waste their lives listening to

Howard Stern." I guess you could consider yourself normal if you are 103 years old or an engineer or math teacher or something. But then you have to consider how normal can that be?

Dear Wise one: I like to drive the speed limit. Mildred yells at me all the time to speed up. Is this normal?
    Will Knapp, Fever Blister, Arkansas

Dear Will: Yeah, this is pretty normal. Women are pretty much always yelling at guys for something; they were designed that way. It does however sound as though it's about time you turned your blinker off and started riding the senior citizen courtesy van or some other form of public transportation. And if you should find yourself in front of me, please don't be offended if I pull out my shotgun and blast a hole in your radiator. Have a nice day.

Dear Ultimate Arbiter: I have been married now for thirty years to the same man. There have been times when I wanted to kill him, sometimes he smells bad, he's not too bright, and I'm always bailing him out of trouble. However, he's starting to grow on me. In my weaker moments I tolerate him pretty easily, and sometimes I kind of like him. Is this normal?
    Mildred Weedlemore, Varicose, Fla.

Dear Mildred: Whenever you have one of those moments, close your eyes, take a deep breath, and the moment will pass.   If you ever get to the point where these feelings persist, take a couple of estrogen pills and seek professional help.

Dear Omniscience: What should I do when I come to a door and the sign says, "ꓶꓶՈ◖"?
Walter Mellen, Skunkbath, Ut.

Dear Judge: This morning when I got up I went into the kitchen.   I startled my wife, who at the time was concentrating, frying omelets on the stove.   She was so surprised she whirled around with the pan still in her hand striking me in the face and knocking me unconscious.   Shortly afterward I came to with mushrooms up my nose.   And I was blind, too, until I scraped the medium cheddar out of my eyes.   Then I realized I could no longer remember how to do log rhythms without a calculator.   Is this normal?
Eric Nid, Sheep Dip, Montana

Dear Mr. Nid: First, being married to a woman who puts mushrooms on her omelet is certainly not normal, but I'm sure you already knew that.   Neither is having a frying pan-shaped tattoo embossed on your face or understanding log rhythms.   The good news is you are now a victim, so you can feel normal going through life feeling miserable and being picked on, seeking federal aid and relief through the courts anytime you have something unpleasant happen to you, even if you deserve it.   The rest of us should be so lucky.

Dear Omniscience: I have been married to the same woman for thirty years. She criticizes my personal hygiene unmercifully, helps me drive, and second guesses all my decisions. In spite of all this, I kind of like her, and I don't even philander. Is this normal?

Joe Weedlemore, Varicose, Fla

Dear Mr. Weedlemore: I sounds to me like you are receiving a normal amount of misery, but possibly missing out on a normal amount of guilt.

Dear Expert: For some reason my clothes just won't seem to coordinate. Is this normal?

Brodie Satva, Godvorsaken, Wyoming

Dear Brodie: Actually, yes. No less an expert than me has trouble telling when clothes don't match. That's why I have decided to start making my own fashion rules. If you want to join my support group, I can explain our made-up fashion rules to you, then you will know what is trendy according to me. After that, we plan to go around and pass judgment on other people. It'll be fun!

Question: I am a Berkley Professor. I live in Marin County. During rare moments when my head seems clear I wonder, "Am I normal?"

Prof. Adolph Putz, Berkley, California

Answer: Unfortunately, if you are a Berkley Professor, you are probably not really a Berkley Professor at all. What you really are is either an Iraqi Terrorist or a rutabaga trapped in a college professor's body. Science is just now beginning to understand this phenomenon. One theory holds that you probably died 10-years ago dreaming of anarchy and government subsidized marijuana. Yes, at the very instant your heart and organs were liquifying from a drug overdose, on the other side of the world, in some wretched third-world country, which you were holding up to your class as a sterling example of a political and spiritual Mecca, some crazed terrorist crackpot inhaled his own Anthrax spores. At that instant his soul was in such a panic to get away that it went roaring through space, bumped into you, and, discovering that you had no soul, took possession of the empty space in your cranium. The rest is history. (No pun intended, professor.)

Dear Normal Expert: Every year I get softer. My formerly steel-like biceps are becoming more squishy and flabby. My six-pack is deteriorating into abs of flab, and I can't see my belt buckle any more. Is this normal?
Will Falter, Puerco Fino, Arizona

Dear Will: I wouldn't lose any sleep worrying about being normal. You've got problems much bigger than that. For example, if you've got that much puddin' around the middle, I'll bet putting on boots can be a real project. The grunting alone must scare away cats for miles and you could throw your back out or have a stroke. As long as you have a pair of shoes you really like, why take them off? Wear your shoes for as many days as you can in one stretch. When the time comes that they absolutely have to come off, times when you're in the airport and the buzzer keeps going off and they finally strip you down looking for the weapon until the only things you're still wearing are your shoes, fall down and act like you sprained your ankle and ask one of the security personnel to remove your shoes for you.

Dear Dr. Normal: For years now I have been a closet Laker fan. Now, I have to get this off my chest. I love to watch Shaq travel while blasting backwards steamrolling the other centers in the league who have position on him, brick his free throws, then leap 2 inches off the ground and jam it home all the while whining that he never gets any fouls called even though he shoots more free throws than any one else in the league. Then, in post game interviews I love to hear him brag about how dominating he is, and to see him and Kobe scratch each others eyes out fighting over who gets to shoot the ball and which one is the franchise player who gets to have the next coach fired. Is this normal?

Jim Shue, Oxnard, Ca

Dear Shue: The question is not, "is this normal." The question is, "is this healthy," and the answer is "No!" Life expectancy for Laker fans is less than 2 weeks and they run the risk of dying even quicker than this by having someone's head lights paralyze them momentarily so they can't get out of the way of the oncoming Volkswagen Microbus, or looking up and having raindrops fall into their mouths and lacking enough sense to look down so the water can run out, and they drown, or getting their wool all tangled up in their barbed wire fences so they can't get away from the coyotes.

Dear Answer Dude: I am beautiful, hot, and boys won't leave me alone. They give me love notes, phone calls, and lots of presents. (One even gave me a BMW, but my dad made me give it back.) I don't know what to do. Is this normal?

Signed, ten-and-a-half

Dear ten-and-a-half: No, this is not normal. A normal person would know what to do. If guys keep bothering you, try this: Grow out your leg and armpit hairs and wear shorts and a tank top. (Just don't travel to Europe because I'm told European guys go wild for hairy women.) Or develop some obnoxious and disgusting habits and go into business selling the gifts guys give you.

Additional Apricot Press Books

'The Truth About Life' Humor Books

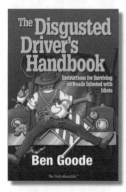

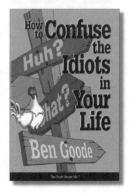

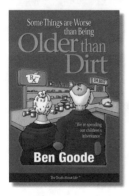

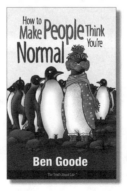

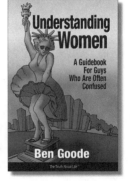

Order Online! www.apricotpress.com

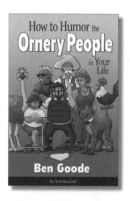

'The American Pantry' Cookbooks

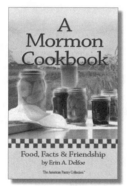

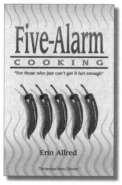

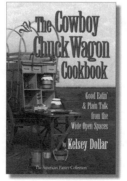

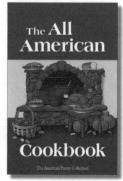

Apricot Press Order Form

Book Title	Quantity	x	Cost / Book	=	Total
_____	_____		_____		_____
_____	_____		_____		_____
_____	_____		_____		_____
_____	_____		_____		_____
_____	_____		_____		_____
_____	_____		_____		_____
_____	_____		_____		_____
_____	_____		_____		_____

All Humor Books are $6.95 US.   **All Cook Books are $9.95 US.**

Do not send Cash. Mail check or money order to:
**Apricot Press   P.O. Box 1611
American Fork, Utah   84003**
Telephone 801-756-0456
Allow 3 weeks for delivery.

**Quantity discounts available.
Call us for more information.**
9 a.m. - 5 p.m. MST

Sub Total = [   ]

Shipping = [$2.00]

Tax 8.5% = [   ]

Total Amount
Enclosed = [   ]

Shipping Address

Name: [   ]

Street: [   ]

City: [   ]   State: [   ]

Zip Code: [   ]

Telephone: [   ]

Email: [   ]